David and the Giant
The Story of David and Goliath

We are grateful to the following team of authors for their contributions to *God Loves Me*, a Bible story program for young children. This Bible story, one of a series of fifty-two, was written by Patricia L. Nederveld, managing editor for CRC Publications. Suggestions for using this book were developed by Jesslyn DeBoer, a freelance author from Grand Rapids, Michigan. Yvonne Van Ee, an early childhood educator, served as project consultant and wrote *God Loves Me*, the program guide that accompanies this series of Bible storybooks.

Nederveld has served as a consultant to Title I early childhood programs in Colorado. She has extensive experience as a writer, teacher, and consultant for federally funded preschool, kindergarten, and early childhood programs in Colorado, Texas, Michigan, Florida, Missouri, and Washington, using the *High/Scope* Education Research Foundation curriculum. In addition to writing the *Bible Footprints* church curriculum for four- and five-year-olds, Nederveld edited the revised *Threes* curriculum and the first edition of preschool through second grade materials for the *LiFE* curriculum, all published by CRC Publications.

DeBoer has served as a church preschool leader and as coauthor of the preschool-kindergarten materials for the *LiFE* curriculum published by CRC Publications. She has also written K-6 science and health curriculum for Christian Schools International, Grand Rapids, Michigan, and inspirational gift books for Zondervan Publishing House.

Van Ee is a professor and early childhood program advisor in the Education Department at Calvin College, Grand Rapids, Michigan. She has served as curriculum author and consultant for Christian Schools International and wrote the original *Story Hour* organization manual and curriculum materials for fours and fives.

Photos on page 5 and 20: SuperStock.

Library of Congress Cataloging-in-Publication Data

Nederveld, Patricia L., 1944-
    David and the Giant: the story of David and Goliath/Patricia L. Nederveld.
      p. cm. — (God loves me; bk. 19)
    Summary: Retells the story of David facing the giant Goliath with a sling shot and his faith in God. Includes follow-up activities.
    ISBN 1-56212-288-6
    1. David, King of Israel—Juvenile literature. 2. Goliath (Biblical giant)—Juvenile literature. 3. Bible stories, English—O.T. Samuel, 1st. 4. Bible games and puzzles. [1. David, King of Israel. 2. Goliath (Biblical giant) 3. Bible stories—O.T.] I. Title. II. Series: Nederveld, Patricia L., 1944- God loves me; bk. 19.
BS580.D3N35 1998
222'.4309505—dc21
                                        97-32480
                                         CIP
                                         AC

10 9 8 7 6 5 4 3 2 1

David and the Giant
The Story of David and Goliath

PATRICIA L. NEDERVELD

ILLUSTRATIONS BY LISA WORKMAN

CRC Publications
Grand Rapids, Michigan

This is a story
from God's
book, the Bible.

It's for say name(s) of
your child(ren).
It's for me too!

1 Samuel 17

Some giants are kind and good. But not all giants! Goliath was a bad one! He roared at God's people and frightened them. You see, Goliath didn't care about God at all—he just cared about his own giant self.

7

David wasn't very big at all—he was just a boy. But David *did* care about God. It made David angry to hear Goliath roar at God's people. Everyone was frightened—even the king and all his soldiers.

avid decided to do something about Goliath. "I'll fight that giant myself," he told the king. "I know that our great God will keep me safe. I'm not afraid of Goliath."

Goliath laughed when he saw David coming. "Why, you're just a boy!" he roared. "Do you really think you can fight a giant like me?"

"You may be a giant and you may have a sword, but you don't frighten me!" David shouted back. "My God is great! My God will keep me safe! Just watch!"

Everyone else watched too. And with just one small stone, David knocked giant Goliath right to the ground. KA-THUNK!

When Goliath's men saw their great giant on the ground, they ran away as fast as they could.

When God's people saw Goliath on the ground, they weren't frightened anymore. For now they knew that David was right. Our great God will keep us safe!

I wonder if you know that our great God will keep you safe too . . .

Dear God, thank you for keeping us safe when we're scared. Amen.

Suggestions for Follow-up

Opening

The story of David and Goliath is a perennial favorite with children, probably because they can relate to the "winner." We must remember that the victory over Goliath was not a result of David's cunning or worth, but the direct work of a great and powerful God. It was David's faith in this God that dispelled his fear of the giant. As you spend time with your group of little ones, look for opportunities to tell the children about our good God who keeps us safe.

As you gather your group around you, tell the children about things that frightened you when you were a child: the dark, loud noises, angry people, thunder. Ask your little ones if these things ever frighten them. Talk abut things that comfort us when we're afraid (perhaps a hug from a parent, a favorite toy or stuffed animal, a song about Jesus). Tell the children that when they feel afraid, they can also remember that God loves them and will always keep them safe. Sing "Jesus Loves Me" (Songs Section, *God Loves Me* program guide) as you gently touch each child.

Learning Through Play

Learning through play is the best way! The following activity suggestions are meant to help you provide props and experiences that will invite the children to play their way into the Scripture story and its simple truth. Try to provide plenty of time for the children to choose their own activities and to play individually. Use group activities sparingly—little ones learn most comfortably with a minimum of structure.

1. Lay out several copies of the prayer poster (see Pattern F, Patterns Section, *God Loves Me* program guide). Provide old T-shirts for paint smocks and a pan of soapy water and paper towels for cleanup. You may want to cover the table with a plastic shower curtain liner and protect the floor with newspaper. Spread a thin layer of tempera paint in a foam meat tray or aluminum pan. Help the children carefully dip their hands, palms down, in the paint and then press them on the paper. You can also make handprints by tracing around the children's hands on a sheet of contrasting colored construction paper. Cut out the hands, and help the children glue the shapes to the poster.

2. Set out dolls, doll beds or pillows, and small blankets. Pretend with your little ones that it is nighttime, and help them put their babies to bed. Talk about how God takes care of us at night, then whisper a prayer or sing a lullaby to the babies. Praise the children for telling their babies about God's care for them.

3. Invite a teenager or another adult to help you and your little ones act out the story. Have your helper take the role of Goliath and stand in the center of the room laughing, taunting, and shouting, "Do you really think you can fight a giant like me?" Rally your little ones around you and have them pantomime David slinging a stone as you call out, "My God is

great! My God will keep me safe!" As the "giant" falls down, invite your little ones to say, "KA-THUNK!" Say excitedly, "My God is so great!" Encourage the children to echo your words. Help the children have fun with this activity without actually touching or hitting the "giant." Remind them that God keeps each of them safe too.

4. Your little ones are beginning to understand the concepts of big and little. Bring a basketful of opposites (big and small balls, books, boxes, trucks, sand pails, and so forth). Spread the things out on the floor, and talk about how the small things are easier for little ones to hold or carry; the big things take bigger hands and muscles. Children may enjoy making a pile of the little things and another of the bigger things. Remind the children that David was small; Goliath was big. But David knew that God was bigger than Goliath—bigger than anything or anyone—and that God would take care of him.

Closing

Help your little ones celebrate God's care for them with this action rhyme:

> God keeps me safe each day. (clap, clap)
> God keeps me safe each day. (clap, clap)
> I belong to God. Hurray! (clap, clap)
> I know God keeps me safe each day. (clap, clap)

— Words: © 1992, CRC Publications

Children will also enjoy stomping their feet or shaking maracas instead of clapping. If you wish, sing the rhyme (music in Songs Section, *God Loves Me* program guide).

Send each child home with a reassuring hug.

At Home

David trusted that our mighty God would take care of him. Point out examples of God's greatness and care in your little one's world— the big bright sun that keeps you warm, the great big tree that shades the sandbox, the rumbling storm clouds that bring tiny raindrops to water the grass. . . .Talk about God's care for each member of your family wherever they are. Tell stories of times your family has experienced an extra measure of God's love and protection—involve older children in a "remember when . . ." time at mealtime. Or bring out family photos, and remind your child that God keeps each one of these dear people safe. Look through your child's baby book, and remember how God has kept your precious little one safe.

Old Testament Stories

Blue and Green and Purple Too! *The Story of God's Colorful World*

It's a Noisy Place! *The Story of the First Creatures*

Adam and Eve *The Story of the First Man and Woman*

Take Good Care of My World! *The Story of Adam and Eve in the Garden*

A Very Sad Day *The Story of Adam and Eve's Disobedience*

A Rainy, Rainy Day *The Story of Noah*

Count the Stars! *The Story of God's Promise to Abraham and Sarah*

A Girl Named Rebekah *The Story of God's Answer to Abraham*

Two Coats for Joseph *The Story of Young Joseph*

Plenty to Eat *The Story of Joseph and His Brothers*

Safe in a Basket *The Story of Baby Moses*

I'll Do It! *The Story of Moses and the Burning Bush*

Safe at Last! *The Story of Moses and the Red Sea*

What Is It? *The Story of Manna in the Desert*

A Tall Wall *The Story of Jericho*

A Baby for Hannah *The Story of an Answered Prayer*

Samuel! Samuel! *The Story of God's Call to Samuel*

Lions and Bears! *The Story of David the Shepherd Boy*

David and the Giant *The Story of David and Goliath*

A Little Jar of Oil *The Story of Elisha and the Widow*

One, Two, Three, Four, Five, Six, Seven! *The Story of Elisha and Naaman*

A Big Fish Story *The Story of Jonah*

Lions, Lions! *The Story of Daniel*

New Testament Stories

Jesus Is Born! *The Story of Christmas*

Good News! *The Story of the Shepherds*

An Amazing Star! *The Story of the Wise Men*

Waiting, Waiting, Waiting! *The Story of Simeon and Anna*

Who Is This Child? *The Story of Jesus in the Temple*

Follow Me! *The Story of Jesus and His Twelve Helpers*

The Greatest Gift *The Story of Jesus and the Woman at the Well*

A Father's Wish *The Story of Jesus and a Little Boy*

Just Believe! *The Story of Jesus and a Little Girl*

Get Up and Walk! *The Story of Jesus and a Man Who Couldn't Walk*

A Little Lunch *The Story of Jesus and a Hungry Crowd*

A Scary Storm *The Story of Jesus and a Stormy Sea*

Thank You, Jesus! *The Story of Jesus and One Thankful Man*

A Wonderful Sight! *The Story of Jesus and a Man Who Couldn't See*

A Better Thing to Do *The Story of Jesus and Mary and Martha*

A Lost Lamb *The Story of the Good Shepherd*

Come to Me! *The Story of Jesus and the Children*

Have a Great Day! *The Story of Jesus and Zacchaeus*

I Love You, Jesus! *The Story of Mary's Gift to Jesus*

Hosanna! *The Story of Palm Sunday*

The Best Day Ever! *The Story of Easter*

Goodbye—for Now *The Story of Jesus' Return to Heaven*

A Prayer for Peter *The Story of Peter in Prison*

Sad Day, Happy Day! *The Story of Peter and Dorcas*

A New Friend *The Story of Paul's Conversion*

Over the Wall *The Story of Paul's Escape in a Basket*

A Song in the Night *The Story of Paul and Silas in Prison*

A Ride in the Night *The Story of Paul's Escape on Horseback*

The Shipwreck *The Story of Paul's Rescue at Sea*

Holiday Stories

Selected stories from the New Testament to help you celebrate the Christian year

Jesus Is Born! *The Story of Christmas*

Good News! *The Story of the Shepherds*

An Amazing Star! *The Story of the Wise Men*

Hosanna! *The Story of Palm Sunday*

The Best Day Ever! *The Story of Easter*

Goodbye—for Now *The Story of Jesus' Return to Heaven*

These fifty-two books are the heart of *God Loves Me,* a Bible story program designed for young children. Individual books (or the entire set) and the accompanying program guide *God Loves Me* are available from CRC Publications (1-800-333-8300).